Facts You Did About:

Lionel Messi

**Written By:
Gerry Bird**

Copyright © 2024 by Gerry Bird

All rights reserved

No portion of this book may be reproduced in any form without
written permission from the publisher or author,
except as permitted by U.S. copyright law.

Table of Contents

Introduction..02

Chapter 1: Career Highlights - Breaking Records...................................05

1.1 One of Leo's Most Legendary Matches.................................12

1.2 Winning Major Trophies - Leo's Most Beloved Cup.........................18

Chapter 2: Playing Style and Skills - Messi's Unique Playing Style.........20

2.1 Training and Discipline - The Physical and Mental Preparation of a Superstar...25

2.2 Overcoming Challenges - The Only Time Messi Has Broken Down..29

Chapter 3: Beyond the Pitch - A More Personal Look into Messi's Life..38

3.1 Charity and Philanthropy - Messi's Magical Matches for a Cause....46

3.2 Global Influence - Leo's Impact on Soccer Around the World..........52

Chapter 4: Early Life and Family...56

4.1 Team Messi: The Family Behind the Football Legend.....................56

4.2 Joining FC Barcelona's Youth Academy...64

4.3 The arrival of a foreign gem..70

Chapter 5: Future and Legacy - What's Next for the Best Player in the World?..73

5.1 Role Model - Leo's Best Ever Interaction with a Fan.......................78

5.2 Leo's Legacy in Soccer - What Will Be Left Post-Retirement............85

Introduction:

"Hey, buddy, wake up!"
Imagine someone is waking you up in the middle of the night out of deep sleep.

Would you know the answer to who is the captain of the current World Cup Champions squad, who also happens to be the current holder of the Ballon d'Or and the current Best Player in the World according to FIFA?

Is it A) Cristiano Ronaldo
Is it B) Kylian Mbappe
Or is it C) Lionel Messi?

If your answer was A or B, better luck next time; but if your answer was C, then let me tell you have impressive soccer knowledge.

Yes! The answer we were looking for is Lionel Messi; the little Argentinian magician who marked a before and after in the world of soccer against all odds.

Also known as "La Pulga" or "The GOAT" (Greatest Player of All Times), Messi is certainly a player worth writing a book about. Not only because of his magnificent soccer career, but also because of his spectacular life story full of hard work and dedication.

So, even if you're not the biggest soccer fan in the world, this book may still be of interest to you as we will embark on an inspiring journey where we will follow the footsteps of one of the planet's most influential and persevering individuals.

Besides, in every chapter of this book you will find engaging trivia-type activities that will not only keep you entertained and hooked to the reading but will also test your Messi/soccer knowledge greatly.

So, if this sounds like fun to you, join us on this tale of a little boy who had everything against him but never gave up on his dreams, just like you, who are reading this, never should!

Are you ready? Then, let's kick off!

Chapter 1:
Career Highlights - Breaking Records

Born with a magical touch for the ball, Messi's journey was destined for greatness ever since he put on his first soccer boots. As he grew, so did his extraordinary skills, and luckily for them, he chose FC Barcelona as the place where to showcase his ability.

His nimble feet and incredible goal-scoring ability quickly captured the hearts of soccer fans around the globe. Every match he played he left both defenders and goalkeepers in awe, and in the blink of an eye, he started to break records like a wrecking ball breaks walls!

For example, he became Barcelona's all-time top scorer while enchanting the world with four consecutive Ballon d'Or awards, a magical feat never seen before! However, the best thing about Messi's story is that it shows us that being an awesome player isn't just about scoring goals; it's also about being a kind person and a real friend both during the game and in everyday life.

FACTS you probably didn't know about Messi's record-breaking career:

1- Complete Dominance: Leo is the player with the most Ballon d'Or awards with a total of eight. The closest to him is Cristiano Ronaldo with only five!

2- European Glory: With a total of six, Leo is the player with the most European Golden Shoe awards. A great example of his consistency!

3- The King of the Hill: Messi is, BY FAR, Barcelona's top scorer of all times. Now act like you are surprised.

4- Team-player: Leo not only has the most all-time goals for Barcelona but also the most all-time assists for the club. Imagine being this good and this generous?

5- The Best of Both Worlds: In the 2018–19 season, Leo became the only player to end the season being both the league's top goal scorer and top assist provider. And then he did it again
next year. What!?

6- Wonder Season: In the 2011-12 season, Leo scored an insane total of 73 goals in all competitions. Would you have liked to face Barcelona that season? Yeah, me neither.

7- Magical Year: Leo broke Gerd Müller's long-standing record of most goals in a calendar year (85) by scoring 91 goals in 2012. 40 years had passed until the little magician from Rosario arrived!

8- Pichichi Master: With 8 Pichichi trophies (La Liga top scorer award), he stands at the top of that list, and seems like he won't be going away any time soon.

9- Start Them Young: Messi is the youngest player to represent Argentina in a FIFA World Cup. Do you see yourself playing in a World Cup for your country at 18 years-old?

10- Permanent Class: Leo is the oldest player to win the FIFA World Cup Golden Ball (best player at a particular World Cup tournament) at 35 years and 178 days. Form is temporary, but class is permanent!

11- Dear Homeland: Messi is Argentina's all-time top goalscorer (106) and player with most caps (180). ¡Vamos!

12- Qualification or Training Matches?: In CONMEBOL qualification matches with Argentina, Leo has the most assists (10) and the most goals (31) for a player. Making every Argentinian proud!

13- Coming in Clutch: Messi has the most Man of the Match awards won in a single FIFA World Cup with 5, in 2022. Talk about coming in clutch during important matches!

14-Taking the Ball Home: Leo is the player with the most hat-tricks in La Liga with 36. Which is crazy considering many players end their professional careers without scoring one single hat-trick.

15-Champions League = Messi League: After playing only 123 matches, Leo had scored 100 goals in the competition, making him the fastest player to reach that sum. Always a scoring threat!

16- FIVEtastic: Leo holds the record for the most goals scored in a single UCL match with 5 against Bayer Leverkusen on March 7th, 2012. You should look for those highlights on YouTube, just saying.

17- Classic Messi: He has the most goals scored in "El Clásico" matches (matches between FC Barcelona and Real Madrid) with 26.

18- Consistency is Key: Scoring 40+ goals in 12 consecutive seasons, Leo is the only player in history to achieve such a thing. More than 500 goals within that span!

19- Brought for Everyone: Showing true constancy in the 2012-13 season, Leo became the first player ever to score consecutively against all teams in a professional league. Sorry, everyone!

20- Can't Touch This: on April 29th, 2008, Leo became the player with the most dribbles completed in a UEFA Champions League match with 16 against Manchester United. Poor guys on the Man U defense that night.

1.1- One of Leo's Most Legendary Matches

Cast your mind to that incredible afternoon of April 2017 in the Santiago Bernabeu Stadium, Madrid. It was Matchday 36 of the La Liga, and Barcelona desperately needed a victory against Real Madrid to stay in the battle for the trophy. The match was fierce, a battle between two soccer kingdoms, but Messi had a secret weapon – his extraordinary talent.

It wasn't an easy match for Messi, especially after the 20th minute when a malicious elbow hit from Marcelo cut Messi's lip and caused some serious bleeding during several minutes. However, this wouldn't stop Messi but rather fuel and push him to an out-of-this-world performance.

Leo scored a beauty of a goal to tie the game at 1 on the 33rd minute, but he was saving the best for last. In a moment that would be etched in the history of soccer, Messi conjured a goal that would decide the fate of the match. The ball danced at his feet, and with a swift kick, he scored a magnificent goal, unleashing joy among his teammates and traveling fans.

But the magic didn't end there. Messi, with a gleam in his eye, celebrated in a way that would become legendary. Like a superhero revealing his emblem, Messi took off his jersey and held it high with both hands for the Bernabeu and world to see. A truly unforgettable moment that will forever stay in the memory of every Messi fan, and soccer fan in general!

Trivia alert —True or False

1- Messi scored in every game of his career.
2- He has never won a trophy with Argentina.
3- Leo is Barcelona's all-time top scorer.
4- Bayern Munich is the rival Leo scored five goals against in a single UCL match.
5- Leo won the Sextuple with Barcelona in 2009.
6- His biggest rival during his time in La Liga was Cristiano Ronaldo.
7- He never scored a hat-trick against Real Madrid
8- Messi continues to be Argentina's youngest ever player to debut at a World Cup
9- He has never scored a hat-trick in a World Cup match.
10- Leo has never won the Champions League trophy.
11- The record for most goals in El Clásico matches is currently held by him.
12- Messi holds the record for the longest scoring streak in La Liga (21 games).
13- He is the current holder of the Ballon d'Or trophy.
14- Messi scored the winning goal in the 2009 FIFA Club World Cup Final against Estudiantes de la Plata.
15- Messi scored 91 goals in the calendar year 2020.

16- Leo is the UEFA Champions League all-time top scorer.

17- He has never scored a free kick.

18- Lionel holds the record for most goals for a single club.

19- He didn't win any trophies at PSG.

20- Messi played a crucial role in helping Inter Miami winning their first ever trophy.

Correct answers True (T), False (F): 1. F; 2. F; 3. T; 4. F; 5. T; 6. T; 7. F; 8. T; 9. T; 10. F; 11. T; 12. T; 13. T; 14. T; 15. F; 16. F; 17. F; 18. T; 19. F; 20. T.

Bonus Questions —Who Am I?

21- Together with Leo and Neymar we formed the reckless trio known as the MSN that won everything there is to win. I'm also one of Leo's dearest friends and I'm soon joining him at Inter Miami. Who am I?

22- Although I wasn't his first coach at a professional level, I was the most influential coach during his first years and helped him take his skills to the next level. Who am I?

23- I am a German soccer player who scored 85 goals in the year 1972 and thought for sure this was a record that was never going to be broken.
Until Messi arrived. Who am I?

24- I am an Argentinian legend who has always been compared to Leo. I am also a skillful left-footed player who played for Barcelona and helped the Argentinian National team win the World Cup trophy as well. Who am I?

25- I played with Leo in La Masía and was always afraid he got put up against me. Although I started my professional career in England, I soon came back to Barcelona where I played with Messi, won over 20 trophies together, and turned into one of his best friends. Who am I?

Correct answers: 21. Luis Suárez; 22. Pep Guardiola; 23. Gerd Müller; 24. Diego Maradona; 25. Gerard Piqué.

1.2- Winning Major Trophies - Leo's Most Beloved Cup

As you guys have already seen, Leo won almost every trophy he could possibly win with Barcelona. However, there was one trophy missing from his collection, and that is the World Cup trophy. Winning a World Cup is like the ultimate dream for a soccer player, and for Messi, it was even more special because he got close several times, but it always remained elusive.

When Argentina won the World Cup in 2022, it was like a fairy tale come true for Messi. It wasn't just a victory for his team, it was a triumph for him, with an even sweeter taste as he and his teammates had put the name of Argentina on the top of the world once again. Imagine working super hard for years for something you really, really want, and then finally getting it; well that satisfaction is just what Messi felt.

Leo has said before that there are many trophies in his cabinet, but none like this one. This trophy means a lot to him as it represents his childhood dream fulfilled, but also the feeling that, even when things seem impossible, there is always a way to overcome difficulties with enough hard work, discipline, and love for what you do. And I hope this story inspires you to pursue your goals, to believe in yourself and to never give up, no matter how difficult the road may seem.

Chapter 2:
Playing Style and Skills - Messi's Unique Playing Style

After seeing Messi play, one can easily imagine him as a superhero with special powers. You can immediately tell that he is at least one level above everyone else, especially when it comes to dribbling as it is one of his most noteworthy skills. With the ball stuck to his feet, he can dance past opponents like they're not even there, and just with subtle body movements he
can scatter defenders around the pitch.

Remember what he did to Boateng back in 2015 (one of the best defenders in the world at the moment) in a UEFA Champions League Semifinal match? That's the perfect sample of Messi's career: wizardly movement and phenomenal finishing, all in a matter of seconds; simply magnificent!

However, what truly makes Messi really special is his teamwork. He's like the greatest friend you've ever had as he's always caring for his teammates, passing the ball and helping them score too. Imagine playing with your friends and sharing the joy of soccer with them – that's Messi on the soccer field!

FACTS you probably didn't know about Messi:

1- Dribbling Maestro: Although he has scored hundreds and hundreds of goals, Messi is better known for his mesmerizing dribbling skills. He can weave through defenders like a slalom skier, making it look effortless!

2- Mastermind Coach: Pep Guardiola changed Messi's playstyle and vision of the game completely by constantly making him switch positions and roles on the field. What a tactical genius!

3- A Blessing in Disguise: Although he had to fight against a Growth Hormone Disease, Messi's short stature is in fact what has helped him be so good at soccer as his lower center of gravity makes it easier for him to change direction quickly and maintain balance, leaving defenders in awe.

4- Left-Footed Magic: While Messi does his magic on the field mostly with his left foot, he is actually right-handed. Just watch him signing autographs to fans and you will see!

5- From 0 to 100 Real Quick: Another key characteristic of Messi's playstyle is his lightning-fast acceleration. He can go from a standstill to full speed in the blink of an eye, leaving defenders struggling to keep up.

6- Game Recognizes Game: Following his very first training session with Barcelona and after seeing just a bit of his skills, Ronaldinho told everyone Messi was going to be the best player in the world one day. Imagine how good that must have felt for Messi!?

7- Like Two Grains of Rice: Leo has constantly been compared to Maradona, especially after he scored similar goals to two of Maradona's most famous goals; He replicated "The Hand of God" and the "1986 Goal of the Century" against Espanyol and Getafe respectively, both of them in 2007.

8- Came to Rescue Us: At the early age of 20 years-old, Messi received the nickname of "Messiah" from the Spanish media after his showcase of abilities and skills. Talk about hype!

9- "El Payasito": Although his name wasn't as popular as others, Messi has said that his idol growing up was Pablo "El Payasito" Aimar. He says he always liked the way he played and that he wanted to play just like him.

10- One of Us: Despite having out-of-this-world skills and abilities since birth, Messi has never failed to assist team practices and drills. His gift came from heaven, but he still has got to work on it!

2.1- Training and Discipline - The Physical and Mental Preparation of a Superstar

In order to continue being the best player in the world, Messi takes really good care of his body. He engages in workouts designed to enhance his muscle strength and flexibility, just like stretching before playing your favorite game to avoid feeling stiff. And guess what? Messi loves playing different sports like basketball and tennis to keep his body active and fit.

However, being a soccer superstar isn't just about physical strength; it's also about having a strong mind. Do you imagine what it feels like to have tens of thousands of people booing you while playing? That can certainly affect most players, but hey, not Messi!

Leo practices on focusing and staying calm in tough situations by doing things like deep breathing and visualizing success prior to every match. He visualizes scoring goals and winning games, just like you might imagine yourself going on a date with your crush after trying many times. Messi believes in himself and stays positive, and that's a big part of what makes him a superstar!

Trivia alert —Fill in the Blanks

1- Messi grew up idolizing another Argentinian player who happened to win the World Cup with him in 2022 as Assistant Coach. His name is _____ _____.

2- Leo started his career playing on the left wing. He then transitioned to the right wing, but found his best place playing on the _____ _____ position.

3- Apart from soccer, Leo often plays other sports like _____ and _____.

4- While they are both great players, Cristiano and Messi differ a lot on their playstyles. While Cristiano is more about strength and power, Leo is more about _____ and _____.

5- Despite scoring some of the most beautiful goals ever seen, Leo is yet to win the Puskas Award, which is a prize given to the _____ _____ of the season.

6- One of Messi's most iconic moves came in the UCL semi-final against _____ _____ where completely humiliated Jerome Boateng with a dribble and then chipped the ball over the goalkeeper Manuel Neuer.

7- Just like most athletes, Leo's diet to stay fit and healthy revolves mostly around fresh _____ and _____.

8- Leo continues to grace us with his extraordinary skills and abilities even till today, at the age of _____ years-old.

9- Messi's strong and winning mentality earned him the role of Barcelona's captain at the early age of 25, during the _____-_____ season.

10- Messi's signature move is a simple yet very effective _____ _____.

Correct answers: 1. Pablo Aimar; 2. Center Forward; 3. Tennis - Basketball; 4. Dribbling - Precision; 5. Best Goal; 6. Bayern Munich; 7. Fruits - Vegetables; 8. 36; 9. 2012-13; 10. Body faint.

2.2 Overcoming Challenges - The Only Time Messi Has Broken Down

As we have mentioned before, Messi is a very strong guy both physically and mentally. However, back in 2016, Messi hit what seemed to be rock bottom after losing a second consecutive Copa America Final against neighbor rivals Chile, which really hurt the Argentinian team, but especially Messi, who was being treated very badly by the Argentinian media and press.

Not even after the World Cup loss against Germany in 2014 left us a Messi so heartbroken like this time as you could see him crying on the pitch with a blank stare. You see, Messi had been playing for Argentina for many years, and winning the Copa America was one of his big dreams. Unfortunately, they lost, and people started to blame him for it, which is why he decided to step aside from international soccer.

The decision shocked a lot of people, but Messi explained that he was feeling really sad about not winning, and he needed some time to think. It was a challenging time for him, and many fans hoped he would come back to play for Argentina someday. And you know what? Messi did return to the national team because he loves representing his country, and well, we already know how great that turned out: Copa América plus World Cup!

So, now you know that even superstars like Messi can feel sad and disappointed, and it's okay to step back, take a break, and try again later. Messi showed that it's important to prioritize your mental health and make decisions that are best for you, even if they surprise others.

Trivia alert —Multiple Choice Questions

1- Which of these numbers has Messi not worn for Barcelona?
A) 19 B) 30 C)10 D) 11

2- How much did Paris Saint Germain pay Barcelona for Lionel Messi in 2021?
A) $100 Million B) $1 Million C)$10 million D) Nothing.

3- What brand of soccer boot does he endorse?
A) Adidas B) Nike C) Puma D) Under Armour

4- What medical condition did Leo suffer from as a youth?
A) Asthma B) Growth Hormone Deficiency
C) Chickenpox D) Covid

5- What is Leo's full name?
A) Luis Andrés Messi   B) Leonardo Messi C) Lionel Andrés Messi D) Juan Andrés Messi

6- Which one of these is a nickname given to him?
A) The midget B) Messiah C) Mess D) The martian

7- Which honor was given to Leo in the year 2007?
A) Ballon d'Or B) Golden Boot C) The Best Award
D) None

8- In which season did Messi surpass Pelé's record for most goals with a single club?
A) 2020-21 B) 2019-20 C) 2022-23 D) 2015-16

9- How many UEFA Champions League titles did Messi win with Barcelona?
A) 3 B) 4 C) 2 D) 1

10- How many goals did Messi score in his first official season with Barcelona's first team?
A) 20 B) 30 C) 10 D) 1

11- What other nation apart from Argentina did Messi have the chance to represent?
A) Portugal B) Uruguay C) Spain 10 D) Venezuela

12- Messi and Argentina won the Gold medal at the 2008 Olympics. What team did they beat in the final?
A) Nigeria B) Brazil C) Germany 10 D) USA

13- Leo made his debut for Argentina in a friendly match against Hungary in 2005. What happened 43 seconds into his debut?
A) He scored B) He assisted C) He cried 10 D) He received a red card

14- Messi played the full 120 minutes of the 2022 World Cup Final against France. How many goals did he score?
A) None B) 1 C) 2 D) 3

15- His goal against Atlético Madrid in May 2015 meant a lot to him and his team. Why?
A) The goal gave them the Champions League B) The goal gave them the league C) It was a beautiful goal D) It was Messi's last goal for Barça

16- Messi faced Cristiano Ronaldo for the first time ever in the first leg of the 2008 Champions League semi-final against Manchester United. What was the score of that game?
A) 2-0 B) 0-2 C) 3-3 D) 0-0

17- Under which coach did Messi lift the World Cup Trophy?
A) Lionel Scaloni   B) Alejandro Sabella C) Diego Maradona D) José Pékerman

18- What type of goal was the one Messi scored against Manchester United in the 2009 UCL Final?
A) Header B) Free kick C) Penalty D) Long shot

19- In 2012, Messi became Barcelona's all-time top scorer. Who did he surpass?
A) Luis Suárez B) Ronaldinho C) César Rodríguez D) Johan Cruyff

20- In 2016, Messi became Argentina's all-time top scorer. Who did he surpass?
A) Diego Maradona B) Gabriel Batistuta C) Mario Kempes D) Gonzalo Higuaín

Correct answers: 1. D; 2. D; 3. A; 4. B; 5. C; 6. B; 7. D; 8. B; 9. B; 10. D; 11. C; 12. A; 13. D; 14. C; 15. B; 16. D; 17. A; 18. A; 19. C; 20. B.

Bonus Activity —Chronology Quest

Arrange these milestones in the correct order:

Won the World Cup.

Reached 500 goals.

Scored his first hat-trick.

Won the Leagues Cup with Inter Miami.

Joined Paris Saint Germain.

Won the Copa América.

Became Barcelona's all-time top scorer.

Won the Olympic Games Gold Medal with Argentina.

Moved to Spain.

Won the Golden Boy Trophy.

Correct answer:

Moved to Spain (2004).

Won the Golden Boy Trophy (2005).

Scored his first hat-trick (2007).

Won the Olympic Games Gold Medal with Argentina (2008).

Became Barcelona's all-time top scorer (2012).

Reached 500 goals (2016).

Won the Copa América (July 2021).

Joined Paris Saint Germain (August 2021).

Won the World Cup (2022).

Won the Leagues Cup with Inter Miami (2023).

Chapter 3:
Beyond the Pitch - A More Personal Look into Messi's Life

Yes, Leo is arguably the best player in the history of the sport of soccer, but he is not just great at kicking a ball; he's also a family man and, according to lots of people who are near him, a very good friend as well.

Off the soccer field, Messi spends time with his wife, Antonela, and their three children – Thiago, Mateo, and Ciro, and have lots of fun together, even more now that they are living in Miami where everyday there is a new fun and interesting thing to do.

In addition, Messi is also an extremely kind and giving person as he is constantly working on helping children through his foundation, which focuses on giving proper education, healthcare and access to sports to kids from all around the world. A real superhero inside and outside the pitch!

When he's not playing soccer or spending time with his family, Messi enjoys simple things like playing video games, watching TV, and playing with his dog. As you can see, he is not a Martian, he is a normal person with hobbies, friends and family, just like you and me!

Some facts you probably didn't know about Messi's personal life:

1- Lovebirds: Although Messi married Antonela Roccuzzo in 2017, they have been together since 2007. Their relationship has lasted for 17 years!

2- Family Man: Leo has three sons; Thiago the oldest (11), Mateo the middle-child (8), and Ciro the youngest (5). Is the future of soccer safe with them? Who knows..

3- Animal Lover: Messi is known for being a huge dog lover, now and ever since he was a child. He and his family currently have a pet dog named Hulk (a Dogue de Bordeaux) and another one named Abu (an apricot toy poodle). However, Hulk had to stay in Barcelona due to his advanced age. It was hard for Leo to
leave him behind, but it was for the best!

4- More than Just Soccer: Apart from being a professional player, Leo is also considered to be an entrepreneur, as he owns his very own clothing line called"Messi". Want to dress like a legend? Then you better visit the Messi store!

5- A Lot of Ink: Leo has more than 20 tattoos all around his body, with most of them being about his soccer achievements and family. That way he will never forget them!

6- Short, or Average?: While he did overcome his Growth Hormone Deficiency when he was young, he still didn't reach a great height, staying at 5 feet and 7 inches. Although 5'7" is not that short, it kind of is for a professional soccer player.

7- Loyalty Above All: While playing at his highest level at Barcelona, Leo rejected various millionaire offers from other clubs like Internazionale and Manchester United. Once again Leo showing us love is above money!

8- Second Home: Leo has two nationalities; Argentinian and Spanish. However, the Spanish nationality is just a piece of paper for Messi as he has always loved and preferred Argentina. Loyal even to his homeland!

9- Loud on the Field, Quiet Outside of it: Despite being in the public eye since his teenage years, Messi has always maintained a relatively quiet and private lifestyle. You could say he is a pretty chill guy!

10- Unbreakable Bonds: Although they stayed in Rosario, Messi frequently goes there to visit his parents and siblings. A true family man!

11- Num Num: Messi has recently disclosed that his favorite food is "Asado", which is basically the Argentinian version of a Barbecue. A truly delicious dish you must try if you ever go to Argentina!

12- Not the Only Lionel: His mother revealed that Leo's name "Lionel" was inspired by American singer and songwriter Lionel Richie, who was one of the biggest artists at the time. Crazy right?

13- Then Why Leo?: Despite his name being Lionel, people started calling him Leo because they thought his name was actually Leonel (a very common name in Spanish). He never said anything because he didn't talk much, to the point that he got used to it and even started to introduce himself as Leo.

14- Equally good with the Controller: Leo's favorite games to play when he has the time to sit in front of a console are, unsurprisingly, soccer games like PES and FIFA (Now EA FC). Imagine loading a match on FC 24 and facing Messi? Wow!

15- Bad Financing: Back in 2017, Messi almost went to prison in Spain for not paying his taxes correctly. Then it was found that it was just an accident, and all ended with a fine to him and his dad. Phew!

16- Commercial Legend: Chances are you've seen a lot of Messi on TV, but not only while playing soccer. As big of a celebrity he is, he has appeared in numerous commercials for brands such as Pepsi, Lays, Adidas, Gatorade, etc. Yes, I'll buy anything Leo buys please!

17- Messi's Life Sounds Like..: Leo's favorite music genre is Argentine Cumbia, Don't know what it is? Look for a group called "La Banda del Tigre Ariel". They wrote a cumbia song for Messi and it is legendary. You've got to learn some Spanish before though.

18- Big Dreamer: As confirmed by teammates and relatives, Messi usually sleeps up to 12 hours a day taking into account his night and all of the daily naps. You know, you need a good rest if you're planning on destroying defenders the next day.

19- As Good with his Hands as His Feet: Did you know that Messi plays (very well, by the way) the guitar? He says it is an activity that relaxes him and helps distract him from the nerves of a match.

20- Weird Nickname?: If you hear people calling Messi a goat or see photoshops of him being drawn as a goat, don't freak out! GOAT refers to Greatest Of All Times, and it's a term sports lovers often use with players that are above the rest, just like Leo is!

3.1 Charity and Philanthropy - Messi's Magical Matches for a Cause

As we mentioned earlier, Leo is well-known for having a big heart for helping others. And although he does have a foundation where he focuses on helping kids from all over the world gain access to proper education, healthcare and sports, he also helps particular causes in the best way a soccer player could ever help, by setting up a charity match with other soccer stars and legends.

A great example of this happened in July 2013, where he got together with Neymar Jr. (who at the time wasn't his teammate at Barcelona yet), to play a match in Lima, Perú, with the intent of using all the money they gathered from tickets and merchandise to help vulnerable kids and teenagers of this country, which is one of the poorest of all South America.

Messi called some of his Argentinian and Barcelona friends such as Javier Mascherano, Sergio Busquets, Pablo Aimar, Ezequiel Lavezzi, etc., while Neymar was in charge of gathering a "Rest of the World" team, where he called some renowned soccer stars like Julio Cesar, Marco Materazzi, Julio Baptista, Jefferson Farfan, and others.

The game was all about having fun and laughing with friends (which is always the most important thing to do when you're playing soccer or any other sport), so no wonder why there were 13 goals in the game. Yes, 13! Messi's team won 8-5, and he scored two beautiful goals that game. That's what I call having fun for a cause!

Trivia alert —True or False

1- Messi has four children; three sons and a daughter.
2- Leo has less than 10 tattoos.
3- He still lives with his parents.
4- Apart from Argentinian, Leo is also Spanish.
5- Leo owns companies outside of the world of soccer.
6- His foundation is focused on helping elderly people from around the world.
7- Messi and Antonela named their son Ciro because of an Argentinian singer of the same name that they both admire.
8- He plays the piano.
9- Leo had never been to the U.S. before singing with Inter Miami FC.
10- For every game, Leo wears boots that are engraved with the names of his spouse and children.
11- Messi visits Argentina several times during the year.
12- Leo is a UNICEF ambassador.
13- Messi's favorite music is Rock & Roll.
14- Him and his family own a cat named Leo,
15- He owns a private jet that can take him anywhere he wants, anytime he wants.

16- Leo is in charge of designing the clothes for the clothing store that he owns called the Messi Store.

17- Messi loves watching superhero movies with his family.

18- Besides soccer, Lionel also plays professional basketball.

19- Thiago, Messi's oldest son, is a huge fan of Cristiano Ronaldo.

20- Before marrying Antonela, he was married to someone else and got divorced.

Correct answers True (T), False (F): 1. F; 2. F; 3. F; 4. T; 5. T; 6. F; 7. T; 8. F; 9. F; 10. T; 11. T; 12. T; 13. F; 14. F; 15. T; 16. F; 17. T; 18. F; 19. T; 20. F.

Bonus Questions —Who Am I?

21- I am one of Leo's most beloved relatives as I helped him a lot during his years as a kid. Unfortunately, I didn't see him play as a professional, but he continues to dedicate all goals and triumphs to me, especially that one trophy he won in 2022. Who am I?

22- I am 11 years-old, and when I arrived, I changed Leo's life completely. I see him everyday when he gets home, and he says I'm one of the funniest persons ever. Also, I love him deeply, just like he loves me. Who am I?

23- I am a Spanish soccer player who played together with Leo at Barcelona for 13 seasons and was the first of his former teammates to join him at Inter Miami FC. I tried to convince Leo to play for the Spanish national team but, unfortunately for me, I didn't succeed. Who am I?

24- I met Leo when I was just eight years old and he was ten. My cousin introduced me to him, and we became friends at that time, but I didn't know how important he was going to become to me later. He talks about me all the time and keeps my name on his playing boots. Who Am I?

25- I was Leo's first ever coach and friend, and I'm someone who played a huge role in building his personality and path to success. I worked as his agent during his first professional years, and I couldn't be any prouder of him. Who am I?

Correct answers: 21. Celia Cuccitini (grandma).
22. Thiago Messi (oldest son). 23. Sergio Busquets.
24. Antonela Roccuzzo (wife). 25. Jorge Messi (father).

3.2 Global Influence - Leo's Impact on Soccer Around the World

Messi is so good at what he does, that means, playing soccer, that it is safe to say he changed the game entirely, and for the good. It now can be considered that soccer has been separated into two eras: The pre-Messi era and the post-Messi era.

Want a good example of a big difference between the pre-Messi and post-Messi eras?

Easy, players' height! While there were many players of short stature that played the game before Messi wasn't even born, it was certainly something very rare to see. Players below the 5 feet 7 inches like Messi didn't normally go pro since the game was too physical and they simply couldn't keep up with opposing players in terms of strength.

However, once a tiny little magician from Rosario made a name for himself in one of the most challenging and rough leagues in the world, kids from all over the world learnt that size doesn't really matter to play soccer. They learnt that what really matters is the hard work, dedication, and love you put into the game every single day of your life. If that isn't having an impact, then I don't know what is!

Trivia alert —Fill in the Blanks

1- Leo's hometown is _____, Argentina's third most populated city.

2- After nor renewing his contract with Barcelona, Leo went to the _____ league to play for Paris Saint Germain.

3- Messi is Barcelona's all-time top scorer with a total of _____ goals.

4- Due to his short stature, a nickname often used for Messi is ___ _____.

5- The name of the stadium where Messi currently plays his home games is _____.

6- During his two seasons playing for PSG, Leo wore the number ____ on his back.

7- The coach that helped bring Messi to PSG in the 2021-22 season is also Argentinian and a former professional player. His name is _____ _____.

8- The trio of Neymar Jr., Luis Suárez and Leo Messi tore defenses for three seasons straight; from 2014 to 2017. Together they were called the _____.

9- Messi received a dog as a gift from Antonela in 2016, his name is _____.

10- Before his teammate Gonzalo Montiel scored the winning penalty kick against France in the 2022 World Cup Final, Leo looked at the sky and said: "Puede ser hoy Abu"; which in English means: _____.

Chapter 4:
Early Life and Family

4.1 Team Messi: The Family Behind the Football Legend

On a random Wednesday of June 1987, in Rosario, Argentina, without anyone having a single clue about it, one of the biggest soccer legends was born under the name of Lionel Messi.

Leo, as friends and family call him, is the third child among four siblings, born to Jorge Messi, a manager at a steel factory, and his wife Celia Cuccittini, who was employed at a magnet manufacturing workshop. While they knew that a new baby would change their lives forever, they certainly didn't know that baby would turn them into one of Argentina's most popular families.

Some facts you probably didn't know about Messi's family:

1- Not a Lonely Child: Leo grew up with two older brothers (Rodrigo and Matías) and at six years old got a younger sister, María Sol. You guys with siblings know how fun this can be!

2- A Family that Breathes Soccer: Apart from Rodrigo and Matías, Leo used to play as a kid with his cousins Maximiliano and Emanuel Biancucchi, who then became professional footballers as well. I guess it comes in the genes!

3- Like Father Like Son: At the age of four he joined local club Grandoli, and the club's coach at the time was none other than his dad, Jorge!

4- Loyal Family: He and his family are huge fans of Rosario's club Newell's Old Boys, which is why Leo signed for them at the age of six. A dream come true!

5- Super-Grandma: His grandma Celia used to take him to all games and practices and was Leo's #1 fan since the beginning. There was no stronger bond than the one between these two!

6- Tribute to Grandma: Sadly, Leo's grandmother passed away before his eleventh birthday. Since then, he has been dedicating all of his goals to her by pointing to the sky in a way of saying "This one's for you granny".

7- Down-to-earth, Always: Leo comes from a middle-class and hard-working family, which helped him develop a humble character.

8- Unbreakable Tradition: Every Sunday, the Messi family had a tradition of gathering around to enjoy a home-cooked meal after every game. Do you imagine all the great stories that came from these moments?

9- Change of Airs: When he signed for the Spanish club, his entire family moved to Barcelona. However, then it was just him and dad since the others went back to Argentina.

10- A Historic Place: Messi's family house, which was built by Messi's father and grandfather with their own hands, is still standing to this day. Is this house as magical as Leo's feet? Maybe...

The impact of his grandma Celia

If there's a Messi family story worth going over is definitely the one where his grandma helps him make his debut for his first ever club Grandoli.

One day when Leo was only four years-old, he was with his grandma on the stands of local club Grandoli, cheering on a family member. Messi recalls: "One of my brothers or cousins were playing and we used to go there every day because we are of different ages and categories."

That day, the '86 team (that means, kids that were a year older than Leo) was playing, but unfortunately, they were missing a player. So Celia thought to herself, why not let Leo show what he's got? So she approached the coach and asked him to put Leo in.

"'No, how am I going to put him in the team, look how small he is." The coach said. "You're crazy, he's going to get hurt," But Celia, as stubborn as grandparents are, wouldn't take no for an answer and kept insisting until the coach finally agreed.

Although Leo doesn't recall much from that day, he remembers his grandmother saying he scored two goals and that everyone went crazy over him. So, it is safe to say that, since that day, his journey to stardom started, thanks to grandma Celia.

Trivia alert —Fill in the Blanks

1- Messi started playing soccer at _____ years old. His first club was named _____.

2- Leo is currently 36 years-old. He was born June 24th of _____.

3- He has three siblings. Their names are _____, Matías, and _____.

4- When the whole family moved to Barcelona, Leo was just _____ years-old.

5- _____ were the days the Messi family used to gather around and enjoy a meal together.

6- Leo and his family are lifelong supporters of the club _____.

7- His grandmother meant everything to him; her name was _____.

8- Leo has two family names: Messi and _____.

9- Messi met the love of his life when he was just a kid. His friend and teammate _____ _____ introduced him to her.

10- Thanks to _____ living in _____, Leo had the chance to go on a trial with FC Barcelona and eventually sign a contract with them.

Correct answers: 1. 4 years-old - Grandoli; 2. 1986; 3. Rodrigo - María Sol; 4. 13; 5. Sundays; 6. Newell's Old Boys; 7. Celia; 8. Cuccittini; 9. Lucas Scaglia; 10.

4.2 Joining FC Barcelona's Youth Academy

Lionel Messi's journey to joining FC Barcelona is as unique as it can get. It all started when Messi was a little boy playing for his local team in Rosario, Newell's Old Boys, where he started playing at six years-old.

Some facts you probably didn't know about Messi's arrival to FC Barcelona:

1- Facing Adversity Since Childhood: At the age of 10, Leo was diagnosed with a growth hormone deficiency, meaning he could stop growing and stay the size of a child forever. Do you imagine staying the same size you are now for the rest of your life? No good, especially for a soccer player!

2- Prodigy Child: Prior to joining Barcelona, Messi played for six years in Newell's Old Boys youth team where he scored almost 500 goals. Unless another Messi is born, this record will not go anywhere!

3- Love at First Sight: After the trial, Leo left a great impression on Barcelona's first team director, Charly Rexach, who wanted to sign him immediately, but the club told him to wait. Not cool Barça!

4- Not Classy but Efficient: When the club finally decided to sign Messi, Rexach had no other paper at hand so Messi's first contract was handed over on a paper napkin. No better way to serve it, am I right?

5- Nothing Like Home: Leo suffered from homesickness when his mother and siblings returned to Buenos Aires, to the point his motivation to play was starting to fade. Thankfully dad helped him through it!

6- Nowhere to Shine: Due to rules that prohibited foreigners from playing, Messi only played a few matches with Barcelona's youth team during his first year, most of them friendlies. Imagine having a game's winning card and not being able to play it. What a bummer!

7- Leo the Mime: Since he didn't play much, he didn't talk much either. To the point that his teammates used to think he was mute. But why bother speaking when your feet can do all the talking?

8- The Place Where Stars are Made: FC Barcelona's youth teams are referred to as "La Masía", and they're considered one of the best soccer talent development centers in the world. Seriously, La Masía is no joke!

9- Complete Athletes: While they focus on teaching everything there is to soccer, players at La Masía also go through academic studies. Yep, you got to know your ABC's if you want to play at a high level.

10- Too Much Talent!: In La Masía, he shared time with players that would later become well known in Barcelona FC such as Gerard Piqué and Cesc Fábregas. No wonder Barcelona youth team was invincible!

11- Old Friends: One of the first persons to talk to Leo and become his friend in La Masía was Víctor Vázquez. Yeah, the guy that plays midfield at Toronto FC and helped them achieve a historic domestic treble in 2017.

12- Broken Bone = Broken Dream?: While playing for La Masía's Infantil B, Messi suffered a fractured fibula, which could have ended his, at the time, short career. Imagine a life without Leo Messi? Yikes.

13- Climbing the Ladder: Leo was named player of the tournament in four international pre-season competitions with the Juveniles B, which earned him the promotion to Juveniles A (first team for youth players). He was simply too good for kids his age.

14- Record-breaker: In Juveniles A, Messi scored a total of 18 goals in 11 league games. More than one goal per game, what!?

15- Saint-Messi: Leo also played for Barcelona C (third-team), helping them avoid relegation to Spanish Fourth Division by scoring five goals in ten games. Talk about having an ace up your sleeve huh?

16- Sorry not Sorry: Most teammates of Messi during his time at La Masía admitted they resented Leo because he used to make fools of them with the ball during training matches. But let's be honest, wouldn't you be too?

17- Visionary Coach: Popular former midfielder and Barcelona's coach at the time, Frank Rijkard, was the one in charge of calling Messi up to the first-team in 2003. Way to go Frank!

18- Historic Date: His first-team debut came on November 16th, when he entered as a substitute in the 70th minute during a friendly against Porto. He was just 16 years-old!

19- Many Get There, Few Make it: Messi is one of the few players to pass through every stage of La Masía and make a first-team debut with Barcelona. And in a record time of just three years!

20- In Good Company: At just 17 years-old, Leo was already teammates of world-class players such as Ronaldinho Gaucho, Samuel Eto'o, Henrik Larsson, etc. Couldn't have asked for better role models!

4.3 The arrival of a foreign gem

Lionel Messi's arrival at FC Barcelona's La Masia was indeed a unique and somewhat unconventional story, especially considering the club's traditional approach to recruiting young talents primarily from Spain. At that time, it was not common for Barcelona to bring in players from outside the country, but Messi's exceptional talent was too extraordinary to be overlooked.

Even as a foreigner in a new country, Messi quickly integrated into the culture of La Masia. His talent, dedication, and love for the game set him apart, making it clear that he was a special case, and a special kid. The decision to break with tradition and welcome Messi into the Barcelona family turned out to be one of the most significant moments in the history of the club.

So, if you ever find yourself thinking something is impossible to achieve, just think about Messi, and how he managed to make his dream come true against all odds through hard work and dedication.

Trivia alert —Multiple Choice Questions

1- What is the name of FC Barcelona's youth academy?
A) La Liga Academy B) La Masía C) Camp Nou Academy D) Barça Youth Center

2- At what age did Lionel Messi join FC Barcelona's youth academy, La Masia?
A) 13 B) 9 C) 16 D) 20

3- What was the name of the local team Messi played for in Rosario before joining Barcelona?
A) FC Barcelona Youth B) Newell's Old Boys C) Rosario FC D) Messi's Magic

4- In which position did Messi primarily play during his early years at La Masia?
A) Goalkeeper B) Defender C) Midfielder D) Forward

5- Which famous coach played a key role in Messi's development at Barcelona's youth teams?
A) Luis Enrique B) Frank Rijkaard C) Johan Cruyff D) Tito Vilanova

6- In which year did Messi make his first-team debut for FC Barcelona in an official match?
A) 2002 B) 2004 C) 2006 D) 2008

7- What was the unique characteristic of Messi's playing style that stood out in Barcelona's youth teams?
A) Exceptional passing B) Aerial Prowess C) Dribbling wizardry D) Goalkeeping skills

8- Messi's move to Barcelona's youth academy was influenced by which factor?
A) Financial incentives B) Family decision C) Love for Barcelona D) Random chance

9- Who was Leo's first friend at La Masía?
A) Víctor Vázquez B) Gerard Piqué C) Cesc Fábregas D) Neymar Jr.

10- Charly Rexach offered Messi a contract on...?
A) A phone B) A paper napkin C) A bill D) A piece of cloth

Correct answers: 1. B; 2. A; 3. B; 4. D; 5. D; 6. B; 7. C; 8. A; 9. A; 10. B.

Chapter 5:
Future and Legacy - What's Next for the Best Player in the World?

There is no doubt that Lionel Messi has left a dazzling trail of magic on soccer fields worldwide as well as a permanent mark on the hearts and memories of soccer fans and players all around the globe.

Although his career is far from over yet, it is safe to say that he will be remembered for more than just his soccer skills; he will be remembered as the small kid with big dreams who taught everyone the value of hard work and dedication.

As for Leo's future, he continues to surprise us. His arrival to Inter Miami FC represented a huge change for him after spending over two decades playing in Europe, but it's all like a new chapter in his adventure!

Who knows what records he'll break or what amazing goals he'll score here in the U.S.? All we know is that we should enjoy his magic for as long as we can, and be grateful for living in the same era as him, the Greatest of all Times!

Some facts you probably didn't know about Messi:

1- Fair Player: Throughout his entire career, Messi has only received three red cards, and two of them were while playing for Argentina. This is an extremely low number, especially for someone who has to put up against all kinds of abuse by defenders on every game.

2- Sniper: Messi has scored a total of 65 free kicks in his career. 2 with Miami, 2 with PSG, 11 with Argentina, and 50 with Barcelona. He is tied 5th on that list with David Beckham!

3- There's Still Hope: Although he has said it is unlikely, Messi has not shut the door entirely to the possibility of participating with Argentina in the 2026 World Cup. He could become the only player in history to play in six different World Cups!

4- A Third Option?: While he doesn't actually have the nationality, Leo could have decided to play for the Italian national team since his family on his father's side are originally from Italy, from a municipality called Recanati.
Mamma Mía!

5- Unforgettable Name: Following Argentina's triumph in the 2022 World Cup, baby registrations with the name Lionel and Lionela grew 700% in the country. Yes, expect thousands of Argentinian players in the future to be called Lionel!

6- For the Eternity: People in Argentina paid tribute to Leo in 2016 by creating a statue of him in an important plaza in Buenos Aires. The statue still stands despite being robbed and vandalized several times, especially after an Argentina loss.

7- The First Ever False 9: While the man behind the creation of the false 9 position was coach Pep Guardiola, Messi was the first ever player to execute it, mostly due to his extraordinary ball skills and movement. A true pioneer!

8- He Did NOT Want to Leave: Contrary to what many may think, Leo did not leave Barcelona because he wanted to play for another team; he had to leave because basically the club didn't have enough money to pay for his new contract. He even tried to reduce his wages, but it simply couldn't work!

9- The Good Son Always Returns Home: Messi has said multiple times that he'd love to return to Argentina as a player and play for his boyhood club, Newell's Old Boys. Imagine what that would mean to them?

10- Soccer Forever in his Veins: When asked if he would like to become a coach after retirement, Messi said it is not exactly what he wants, but that he would love to become a sporting director and be in charge of signing talents for a team. I don't know about you but I'd hire him right away!

5.1 Role Model - Leo's Best Ever Interaction with a Fan

Back in 2018, Messi and an Argentinian reporter left us with one of the most heartwarming moments in soccer history. Prior to the beginning of the Russia 2018 World Cup, the reporter Rama Pantorotto had given Leo a red ribbon his mom made especially for him during an interview, and told him that it was an amulet against bad luck.

The days passed and the reporter didn't think much of it, especially following Argentina's results which weren't exactly an example of good luck: a draw against Iceland and 0-3 defeat against Croatia. However, after winning the last match against Nigeria and securing a spot in the next round, the unthinkable happened.

The reporter managed to get to Messi once again, and after he finished his already prepared questions, Rama asked Leo what he did with the ribbon he gave him in the name of his mother, and Messi simply lifted his left leg and showed him he had it wrapped around his ankle.

The reporter couldn't believe his eyes, and his reaction is simply unforgettable! And you know the best part of it all? Messi still has the ribbon around his ankle and wore it when he won the World Cup in 2022. Imagine how the reporter's mom should have felt after that!

Trivia alert —Multiple Choice Questions

1- Why did Messi leave PSG?
A) The club fired him B) He wasn't getting paid enough C) He said he wanted to return to Barcelona D) They reached a mutual agreement to end things.

2- In 2024 Messi will turn..?
A) 36 years-old B) 37 years-old C) 38 years-old D) 40 years-old

3- At what club Messi said he would like to retire?
A) Barcelona B) PSG C) Newell's Old Boys D) Grandoli

4- As of January 2024, how many more goals does Messi need to reach the 900 goals milestone?
A) More than 100 B) Between 100 and 50 C) Less than 10 D) Between 50 and 10

5- What was Argentina's result in the 2014 World Cup when Leo was at the peak of his career?
A) Lost the final B) Lost in the Semifinal C) Eliminated in the group stage D) Won the World Cup

6- What team did Leo score his first goal against wearing the Inter Miami FC shirt?
A) Nashville FC B) Dallas FC C) LA Galaxy D) Cruz Azul

7- Following his recognition as The Best in 2023 by FIFA, how many individual prizes has Messi won in his career (Ballon d'Ors, Golden Boots, and The Best)?
A) 17 B) 27 C) 7 D) 10

8- What was the result of the 2022 FIFA World Cup final between Argentina and France where Messi scored two goals?

A) Argentina won 2-0 B) France won 3-2 C) Argentina won 4-3 D) Tied at 3 and Argentina won on penalties

9- What was the popular Argentinian club that rejected Messi when he was little?

A) Boca Juniors B) River Plate C) Estudiantes de la Plata D) Racing Club

10- What soccer legend handed Messi his most recent (8th) Ballon d'Or at the ceremony?

A) Diego Maradona B) Ronaldo Nazario C) David Beckham D) Andriy Shevchenko

Correct answers: 1. D; 2. B; 3. C; 4. B; 5. A; 6. D; 7. A; 8. D; 9. B; 10. C.

Bonus Activity —Chronology Quest

Arrange these milestones in the correct order:

Joined Barcelona's Youth Team.
Broke the record for most goals for a single club.
Debuted for Argentina's senior team.
Left Barcelona. 2021
Started his Growth Hormone Deficiency treatment.
Won the Treble with Barcelona for the second time.
Had his first son.
Momentarily retired from Argentina's national team.
Won his first "Pichichi".
Lost a World Cup Final.

Correct answer:

Started his Growth Hormone Deficiency treatment (1998).

Joined Barcelona's Youth Team (2000).

Debuted for Argentina's senior team (2005).

Won his first "Pichichi" (2010).

Had his first son (2012).

Lost a World Cup Final (2014).

Won the Treble with Barcelona for the second time (2015).

Momentarily retired from Argentina's national team (2016).

Broke the record for most goals for a single club (2020).

Left Barcelona (2021).

5.2 Leo's Legacy in Soccer - What Will Be Left Post-Retirement

I have said it before, but I will say it again: Lionel Messi changed the game of soccer when he arrived, and it will never be the same again once he is gone.

While the future seems bright for soccer with so many great, talented players making a name for themselves such as Kylian Mbappé, Erling Haaland, Vinicius Jr., among others, there's little to no chance that we ever see another wizard on the soccer field who dribbles past defenders like Messi.

When he retires, his legacy will be like a storybook full of records, awards, and memories of breathtaking goals. But most importantly, people around the world will remember him as the player who showed that even with physical impediments, you can still reach incredible heights with talent, hard work, and a love for the game.

Messi's legacy is not just about soccer; it's also about inspiring people to dream big and enjoy every moment of playing their favorite sport.